T0368985

Tail Waggin' Howlers

Dog Cartoons

Steve Hall

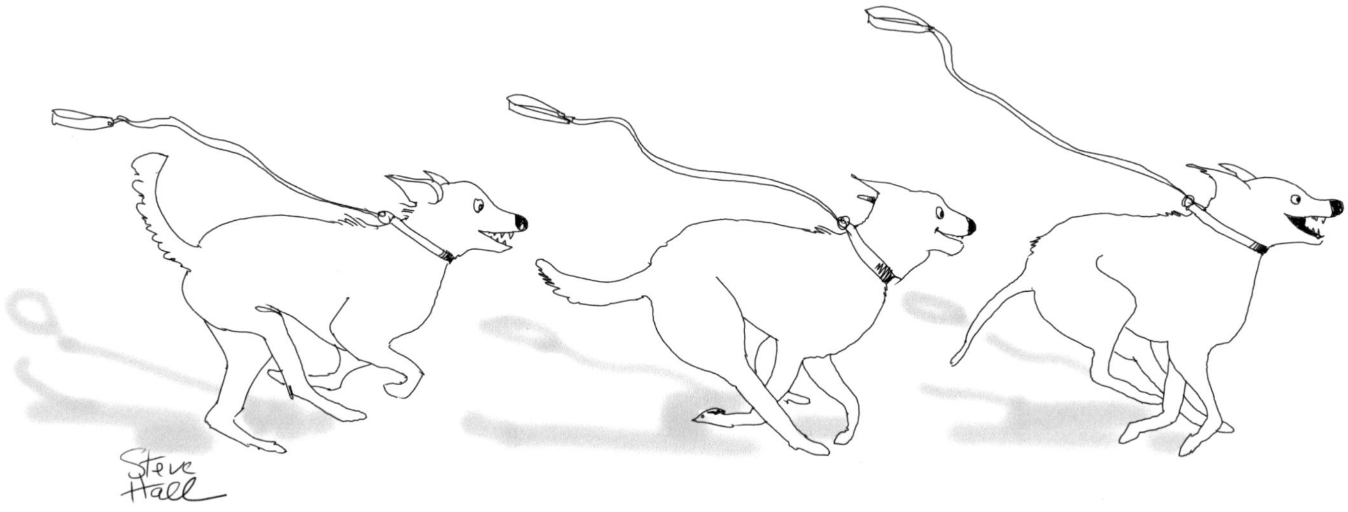
Steve
Hall

Tail Waggin' Howlers

DOG CARTOONS BY STEVE HALL

To Max, Avery, and Harper, my grandkids.

"A book about dogs?
Good grief."

And thanks to writer David Scott for assisting with the introduction.

INTRODUCTION

Fernandina's furry, fantastic, faithful, funny, tail-wagging friends are pampered, petted, patronized, and prettied but not paranoid.

They all realize that their alleged owners are not particularly perceptive.

They don't consider their human caretakers owners, but they let them think they are.

A couple of examples of how this works:

Are you a single guy or gal looking for a date? Simply grab Fido, put him on a leash, and walk a block or two downtown. You'll be instantly approached by cute guys and gals swooning not over you but over Fido. They'll ask his name and tell you how cute he is, petting him and so forth. Once Fido's made the introduction, the rest is up to you, pal. Any medium-sized pooch, from a cocker spaniel to an ugly pound dog, will do. Avoid drooling, snarling pit bulls and growling pugs for this activity.

Dogs are great for getting you out of the house, off social media, away from the kids, and out for a little exercise. A couple taking Fido out for a neighborhood walk will soon be chatting with neighbors, meeting new folks, getting invited to neighborhood BBQs, offered a cold beer, and so much more. Just keep Fido off the neighbors' newly sodded lawn, or things will get ugly fast. Small, barking ankle biters and lawn poopers are not recommended for this kind of recreational activity. Sniffing and marking the wrong household on Fido's part could land him on the HOA's most wanted list.

Want a dog companion but aren't sure you have the required skills? Don't worry; Fido will train you. Humans are easy. Just have plenty of good food, fresh water, and treats on hand.

Steve Hall

"So I said to my human, let me take the blasted cat for a walk."

"*And voila! No one thinks I'm a dog.*"

"I'm watching my carbs, so no bun."

"I have no idea, but the humans give me treats and grog."

5

"He was such an adorable little puppy. I had no idea."

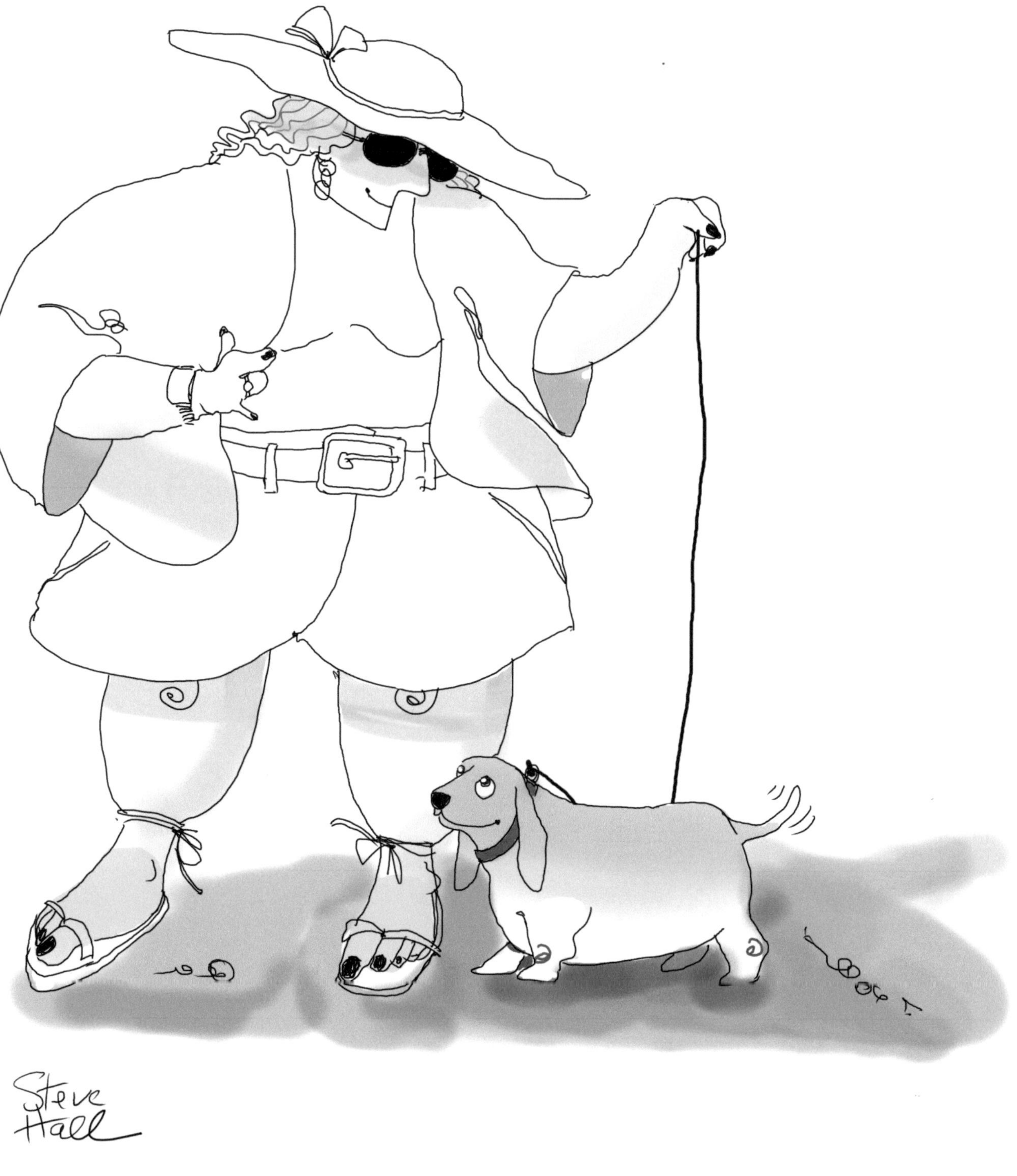
Steve Hall

Shade.

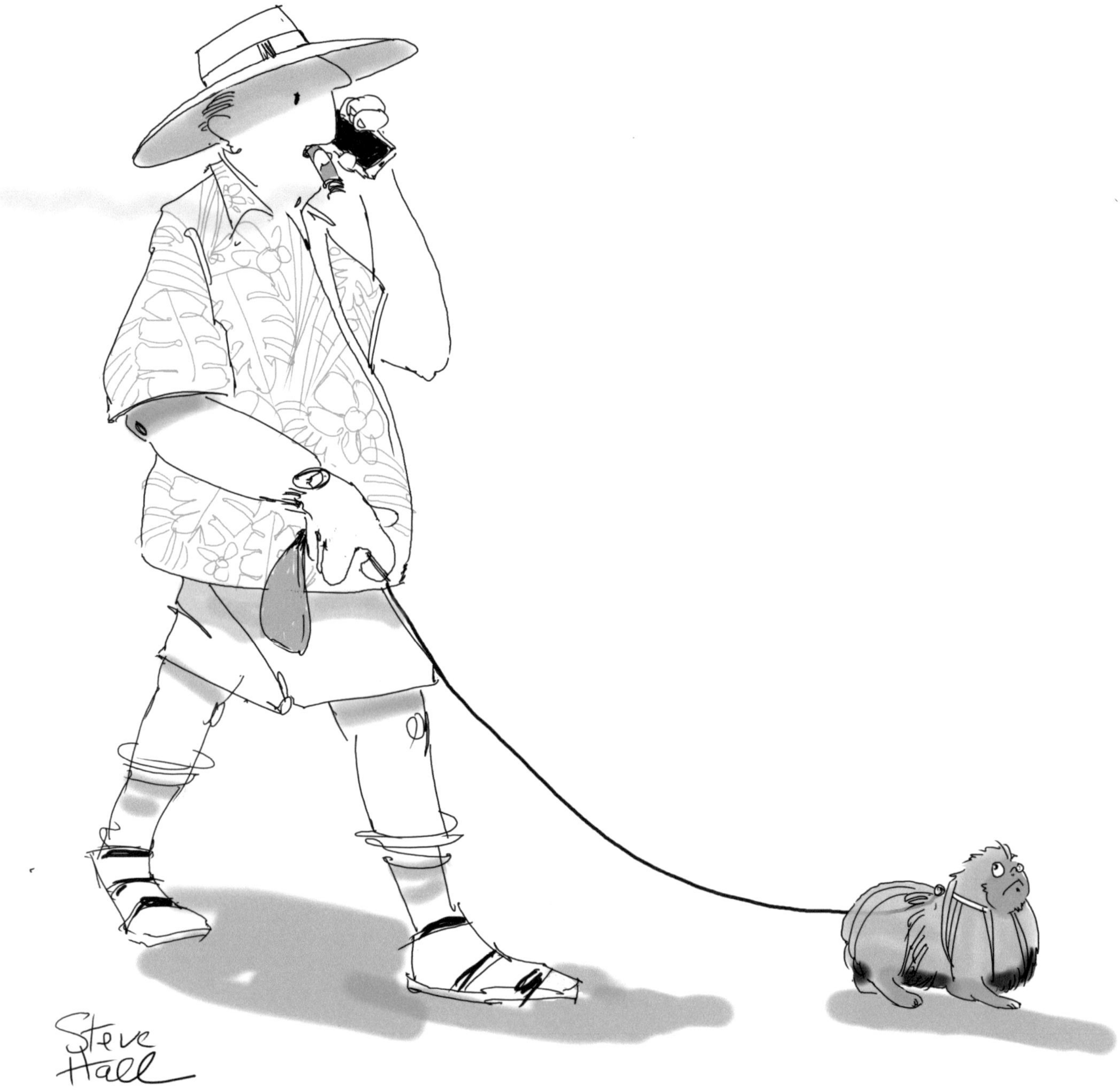
Steve Hall

"My steps were over the top today."

"If I'm not mistaken, that's our favorite beer garden up ahead."

10

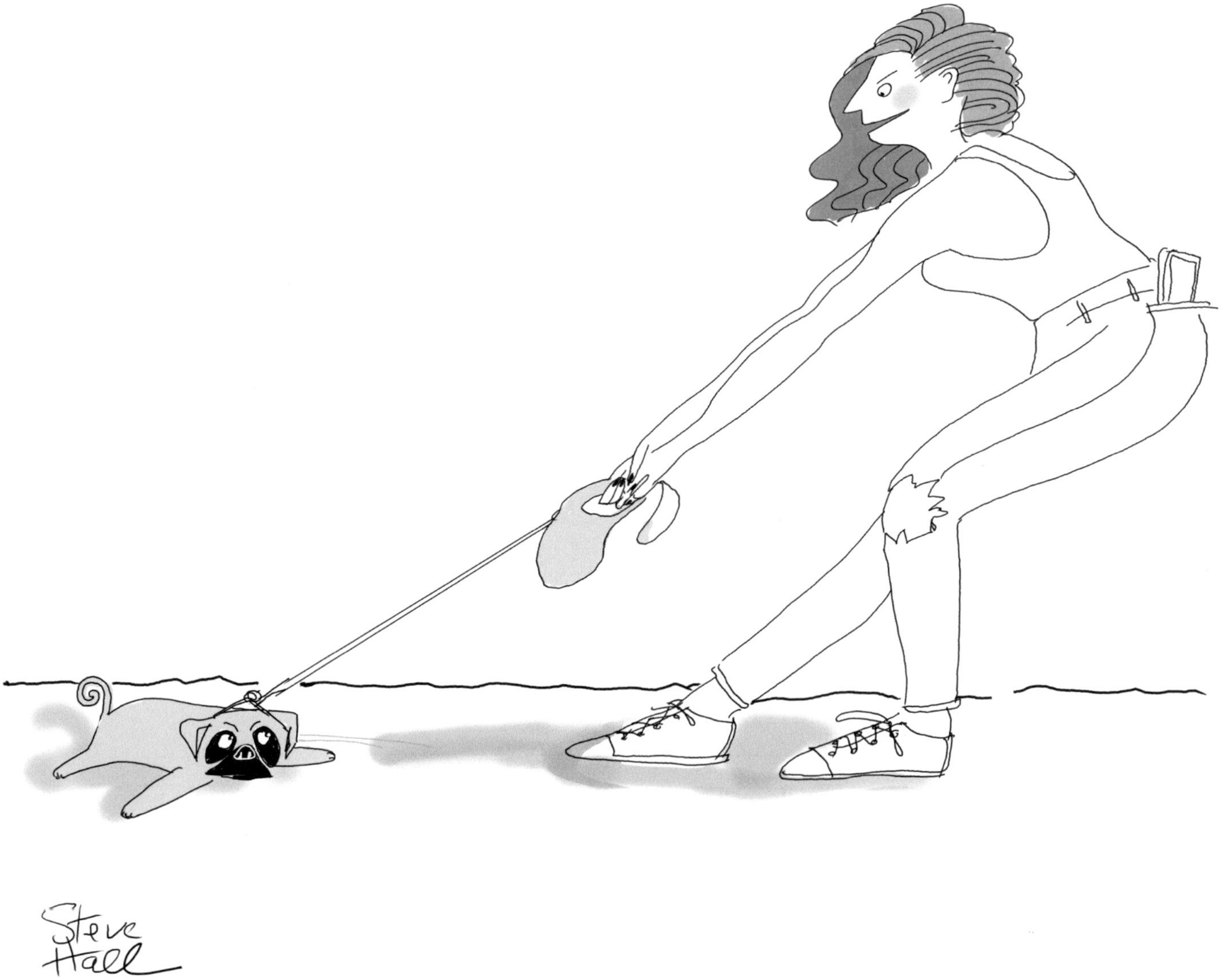
Steve Hall

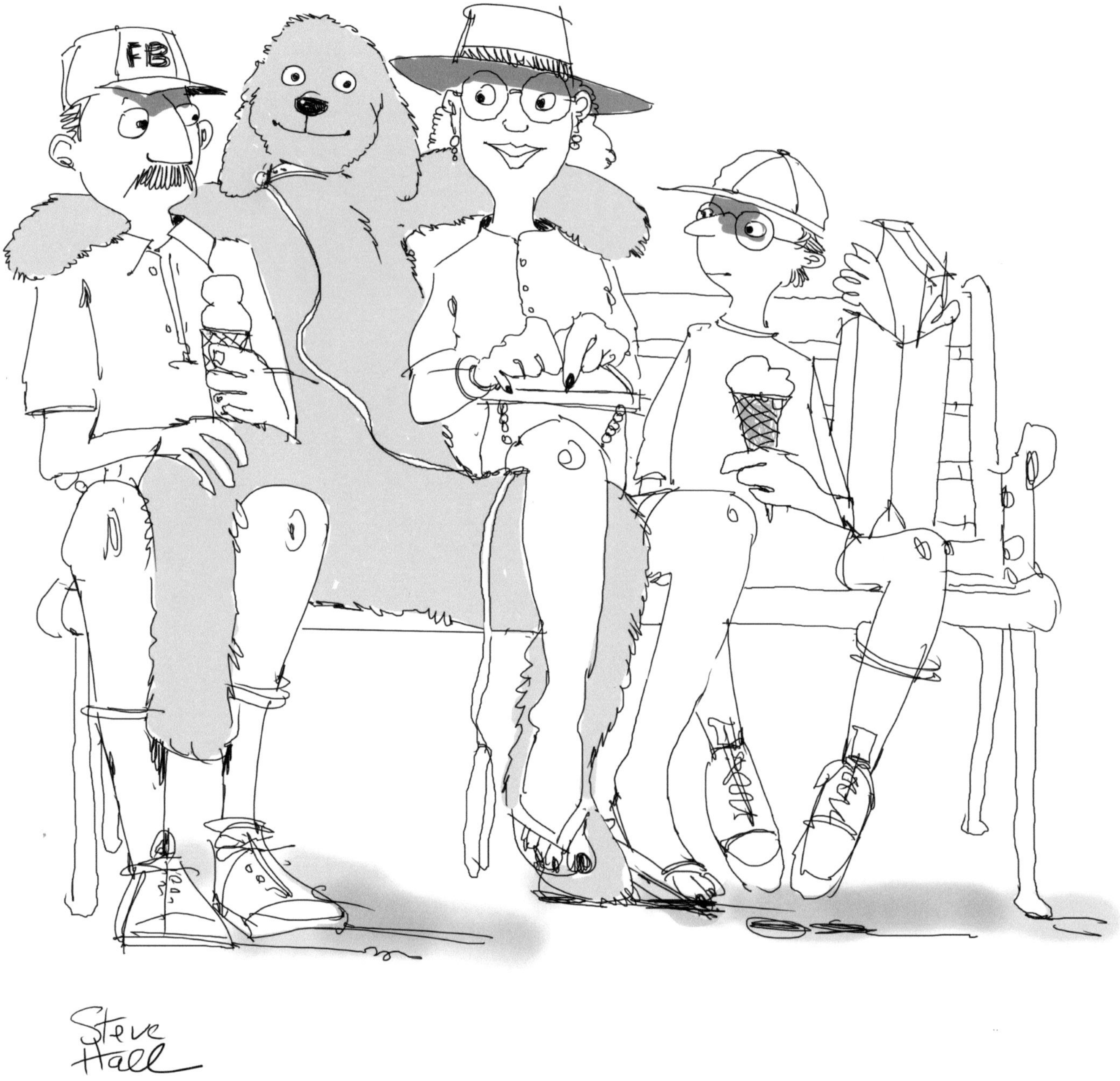
FB
Steve Hall

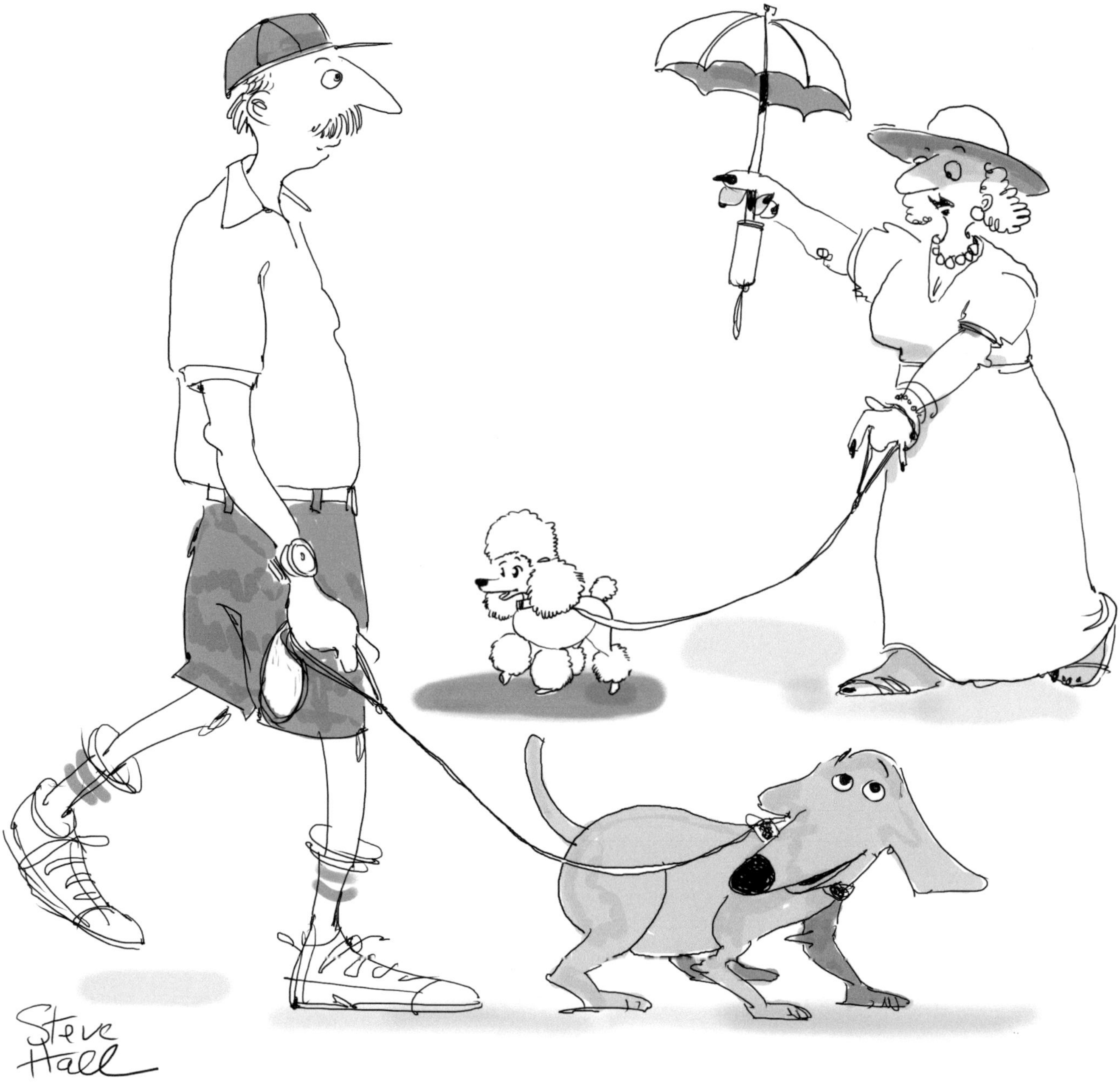
Steve Hall

"Save me, please."

"When you have a minute, please."

"I send them to my groomer."

"Dad, you're embarrassing me."

"Let's see who's forgotten their poop bags today."

"My groomer asked me to pick up my game, so here we are."

"I'm riding my bike! I'm riding my bike!"

Sunday afternoon barbeque.

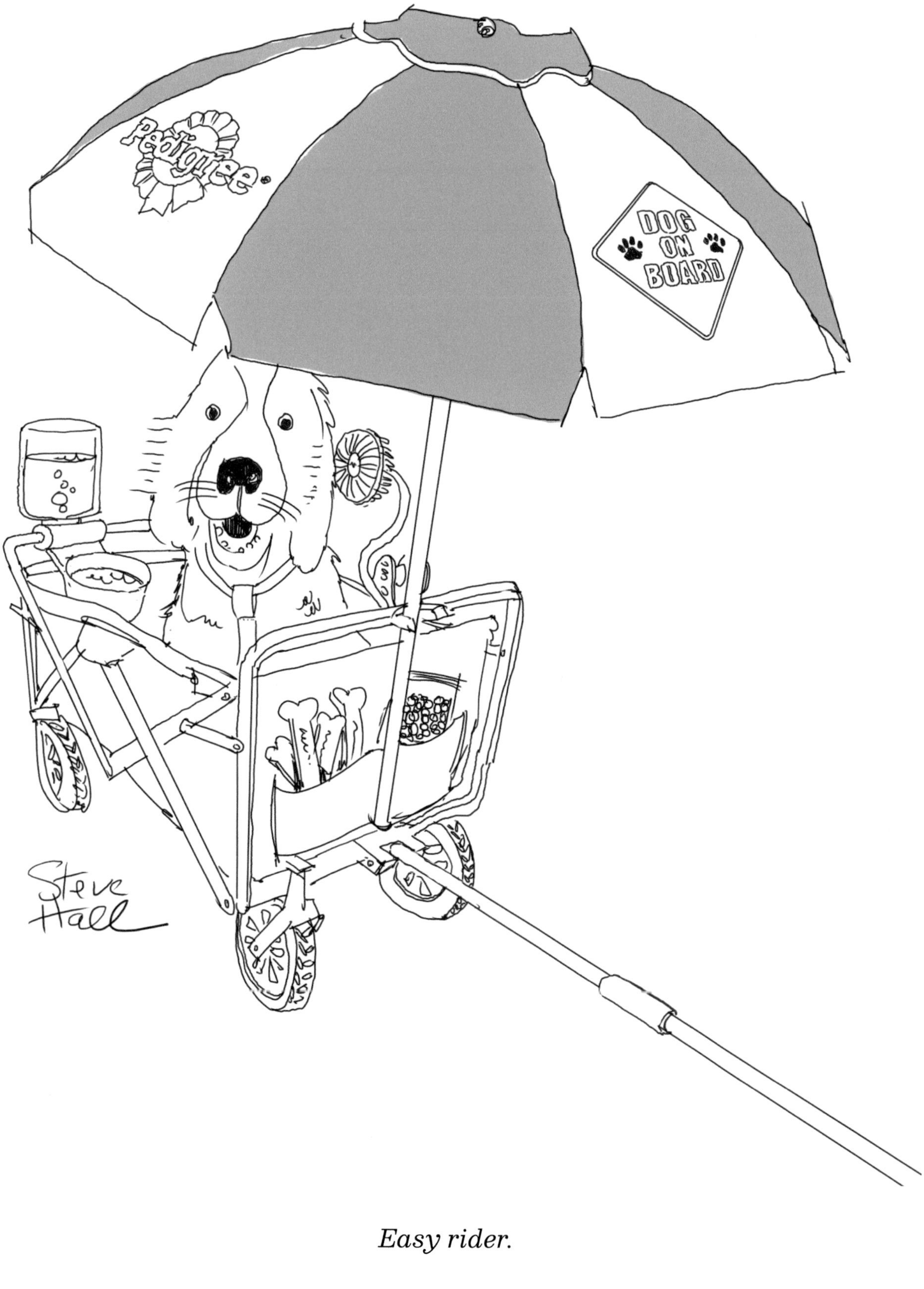
Pedigree
DOG ON BOARD
Steve Hall

Easy rider.

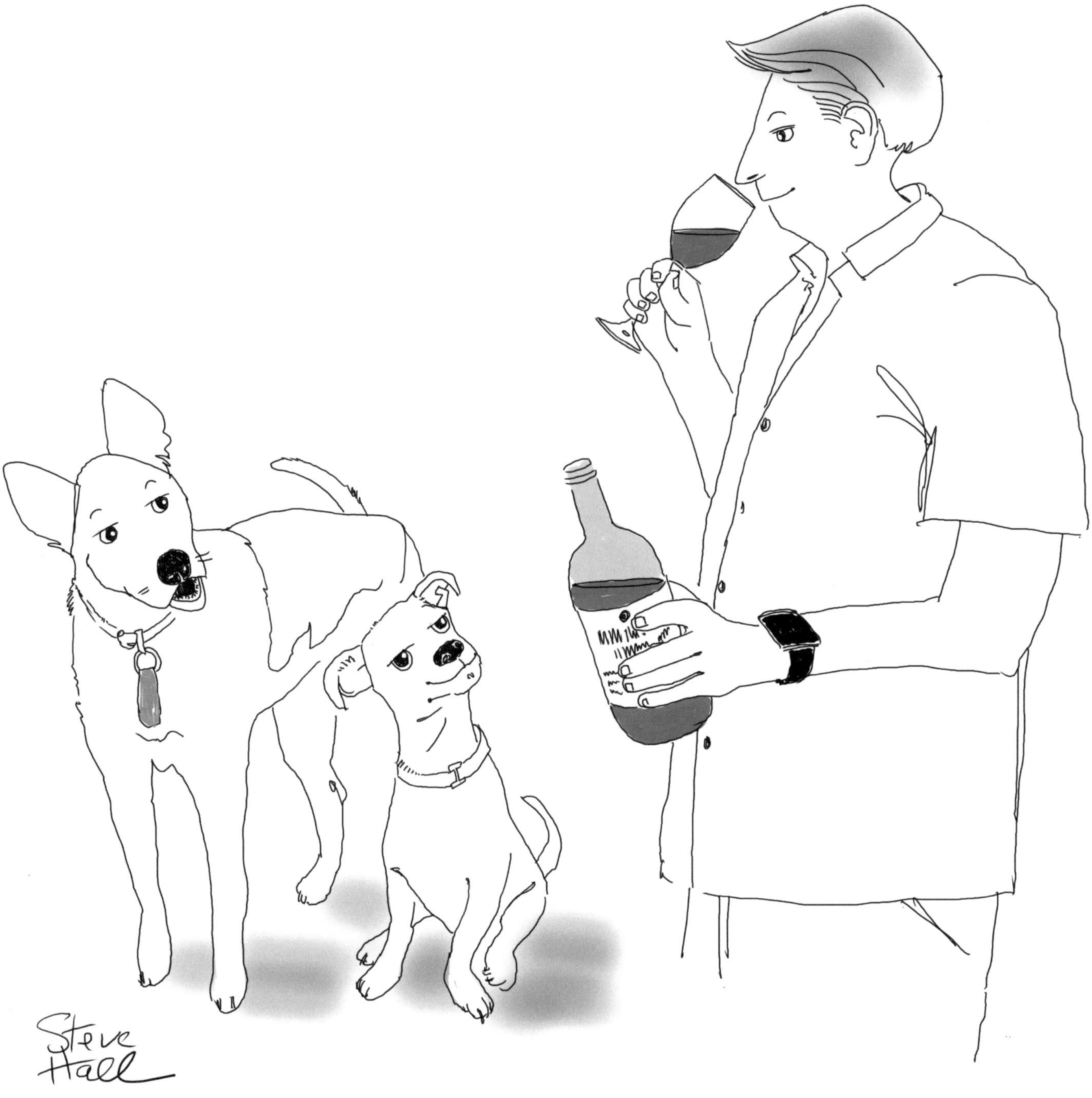
Steve Hall

“Poser.”

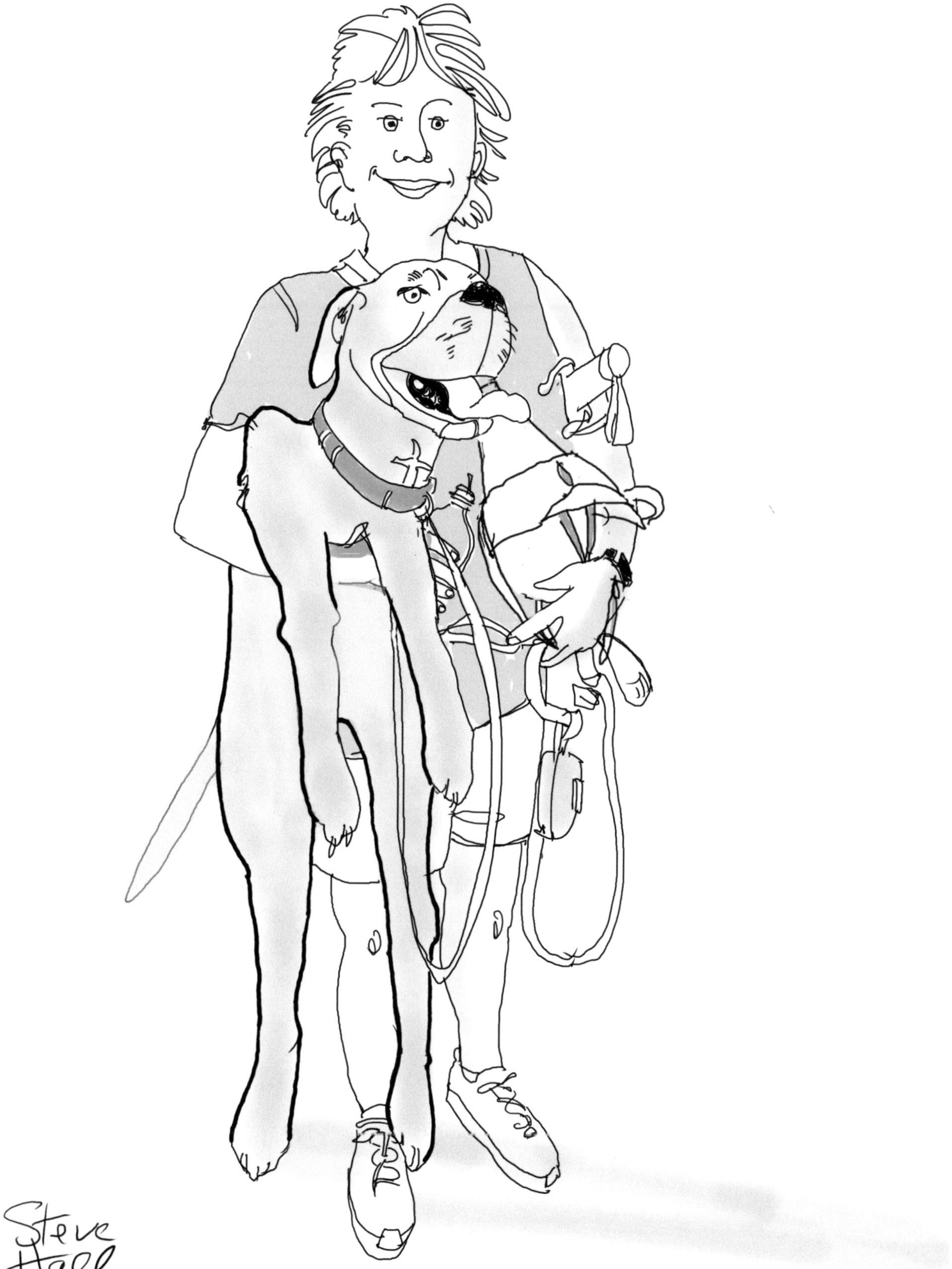
Steve Hall

Dog tired.

"Pals, it's hot out there and cool in here. I tell you, it's a miracle."

"I say let's head to the dog park for some barking."

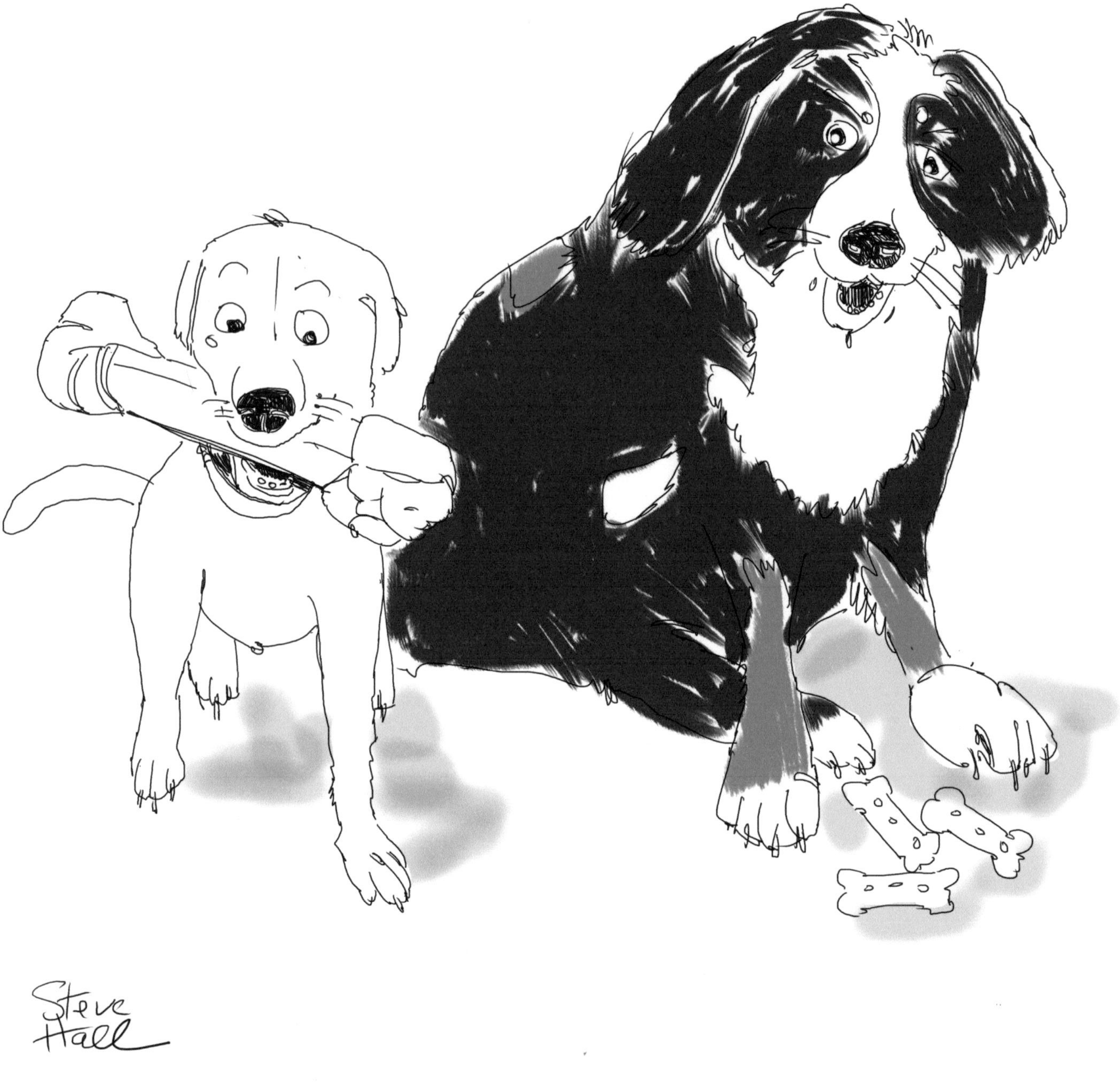
Steve Hall

"Show-off."

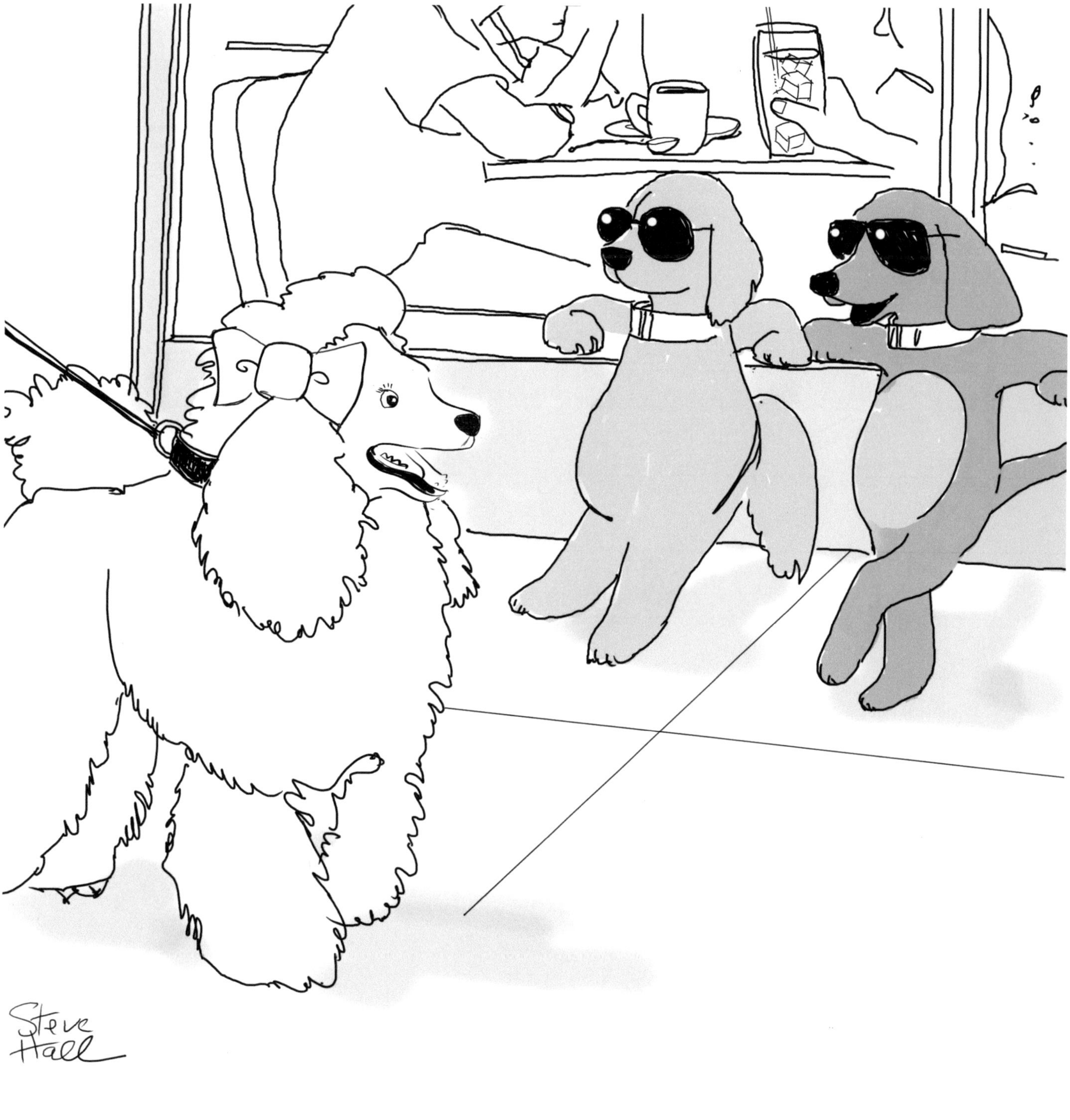
Steve Hall

"Don't stare."

"Ahem! Just a reminder that I'm fully trained, and from the look of things, the puppy may never be."

"And you call yourself a dog."

Copyright © 2024 by Steve Hall. 861568

All rights reserved. No part of this book may be reproduced or transmitted in any form or by any means, electronic or mechanical, including photocopying, recording, or by any information storage and retrieval system, without permission in writing from the copyright owner.

This is a work of fiction. Names, characters, places and incidents either are the product of the author's imagination or are used fictitiously, and any resemblance to any actual persons, living or dead, events, or locales is entirely coincidental.

To order additional copies of this book, contact:
Xlibris
844-714-8691
www.Xlibris.com
Orders@Xlibris.com

ISBN: Softcover   979-8-3694-2682-1
*   Hardcover   979-8-3694-2683-8*
*   EBook   979-8-3694-2681-4*

Library of Congress Control Number: 2024917686

Print information available on the last page

Rev. date: 08/20/2024